About the Author

CHARLES DICKENS
1812 – 1870

Charles Dickens' father was often in debt and finally, unable to pay his bills, went to debtor's prison. So, at the age of 12, Dickens was taken out of school to work in a factory, pasting labels onto bottles. Later he was able to return to school for a time and then work as a reporter covering proceedings at the House of Commons. His first book, *The Pickwick Papers*, was so popular that Dickens found himself famous in Britain and America at the age of 24. Outraged by the terrible wrongs Dickens saw around him in Victorian society, he used his books to urge social change. Parliament sometimes even listened and passed laws to end some of the worst injustices. His readers chiefly loved the larger-than-life comical characters he invented. Many of his books were published first in magazines, serialized week by week. In time, he published such magazines himself.

Dickens had ten children and an army of friends. His hobby was amateur dramatics. He also made a great many exhausting tours, in England and abroad, reading excerpts from his books. Dickens died aged only 58, but is still probably the most famous novelist ever to have lived.

Oliver Twist

Charles Dickens

Adapted by Geraldine McCaughrean

Illustrated by Jeff Anderson

OXFORD

CHAPTER 1

in which Oliver enters a loveless world

For three whole minutes, the feeble object on the bed struggled to breathe. For three whole minutes, no one knew whether he would live or die. If he had died, then this book would be the shortest in history, but he did not die.

His mother did that.

As Oliver took his first breath and began to cry, his mother whispered a few desperate words to the old woman sitting beside the bed, asked to hold the child, kissed him on his small, damp head, then fell back on the pillow. Oliver was an orphan, left alone in a world with no one to love him. The old woman reached inside the young woman's clothing, helped herself to a little something for her troubles, then went to find a workhouse shirt for the baby.

This happened in the workhouse, you see; that most feared place in any town. Only the penniless poor with nowhere else to go in the world turn to the workhouse for help, for it is as dreadful a place as any prison. Oliver's mother had collapsed outside its doors, her shoes worn through, her strength gone, too weary even to speak her name. And so Oliver was born in the workhouse and given a stained old shirt and a second-hand name to wear.

It was Mr Bumble the Beadle[1] who thought of the name. He was working his way through the alphabet, from A to Z, and it so happened he had reached the letter T. So Oliver was called Twist: Oliver Twist, just another worthless, unwanted, wailing waif in an unforgiving world.

Mr Bumble the Beadle put Oliver, for the first nine years of his life, into the care of Mrs Mann. Mrs Mann had such a tender heart that she looked after a whole houseful of workhouse babies. She was paid seven pence a week for each child she took into her home – and seven pence a week is more than enough to feed and clothe a growing child. So Mrs Mann, who could not bear to spoil the dear children, spent only tuppence a week on them and kept the rest for herself. As a result, there was no danger of her little darlings over-eating. In fact many of them gave up and died of hunger (which was very naughty and vexing of them). The rest grew up small and thin, which is all to the good in an overcrowded house.

Oliver Twist spent his ninth birthday in the cellar. That was where Mrs Mann locked up children who cried, and Oliver was a great one for crying. In fact, inside or out,

---

[1] A man employed by a town to deal with petty wrongdoers.

Oliver had been crying ever since the day he was born.

He did not know that it was his birthday, of course, until Mr Bumble came calling and informed Mrs Mann that it was, 'Time for Oliver to go back to the workhouse and start to earn an honest living.'

'You'll be sorry to leave the dear kind lady, I suppose,' said Mr Bumble sharply to Oliver, 'she who has cared for a boy like you when nobody else in the world could love you!' Oliver, his hair still full of cellar cobwebs, gazed up at Mr Bumble's hugely round, red face, and big tears rolled down his white cheeks and in at the corners of his mouth. 'There now! See how sorry he is to part from you, Mrs Mann!' exclaimed Mr Bumble with satisfaction.

The Board of Governors, who ran the workhouse, was determined to save money. Far too many poor people were coming to the door asking for help. Obviously the food was too good! So rations were cut and, from that day on, each person living there received only one bowl of watery gruel each day.

The boys – boys like Oliver Twist – were always hungry. All day they picked old rope to pieces to make wadding,[2] and while they picked, they thought about food. When supper came, there was one swift rattle of spoons on china and the gruel was gone. No need to wash the dishes: they were licked clean.

'If I don't get more to eat, I'll turn cannibal and eat

---

[2] Cloth used to pad or stuff.

one of you!' declared Harry, glaring round at the others, wild-eyed. He looked as if he meant it. 'One of us has to tell them: we need more food!'

'They'd hang us!'

'Or transport us to Australia³ as convicts!'

'Whoever would dare ask?' gasped Oliver.

'We'll draw lots,' said Harry, and held out a bunch of straws like a bouquet without its flowerheads. 'Each boy picks a straw and the one who picks the shortest one will speak up at the end of dinner!'

So that is what they did. Straw by straw, they picked the bundle to pieces. Oliver was left holding a wisp no longer than his straw-coloured hair. The other boys stared at him, then turned away, each glad to have escaped the dreadful mission.

The dining hall was cold that evening. Oliver's breath froze in the air, like dragon smoke. He scraped clean his bowl, then stood up on shaking legs. He walked up to the stove, where the warden with the ladle stood warming himself.

The warden glared. 'What is it, Twist?'

The words seemed to have frozen solid inside Oliver's mouth. He held out the bowl, thin arms shuddering so hard that the spoon tinkled. 'P-please, sir . . . I want some more!'

---

³ A place where criminals were sent to work in Victorian times.

in which Oliver takes up a profession

'More? The boy asked for more?'

The Board of Governors of the workhouse could not believe their ears. Oliver Twist had asked for more!

'That boy will be hanged!' prophesied the fattest Governor, his white waistcoat heaving with outrage. 'Mark my words! That boy will hang!'

Next day, a notice was posted on the workhouse door:

£5 REWARD
for taking one boy
and teaching him a trade
Apply within

Meanwhile, Oliver himself was locked in a cold, bare room and allowed out only to be beaten, washed under the cold tap, and to hear Evening Prayers. Each night Oliver listened, his small heart crumbling, to the other boys praying, *'Oh please Lord, save us from becoming as wicked as Oliver Twist!'*

The notice on the door caught the eye of Mr Gamfield, a chimney sweep. What luck! Mr Gamfield was in need of the money; he was also in need of a boy. (He had been unlucky enough to lose his last three sweeps up chimneys – either burned or suffocated.) Workhouse boys made excellent sweeps. They were kept so hungry that they grew up small and thin: ideal for climbing narrow chimney flues.[4] So Mr Gamfield knocked and Mr Gamfield asked, and Mr Gamfield was given Oliver Twist. All that remained was for master and boy and Beadle to go before a magistrate who would sign the papers and make the whole arrangement legal.

'Does the boy *want* to be a chimney sweep?' asked the magistrate. 'It is nasty work, I understand.'

'Longs to be one, sir!' exclaimed Mr Bumble. 'Ever since he was born it's been his greatest ambition! Indeed, I believe that if we was to make him do any other kind of work, he would run away or die of a broken heart!'

The magistrate picked up his pen and peered about for the inkwell. Quite by chance, his bleary eye happened to fall on Oliver's small, white, terrified face, which rose just above the edge of the desk. 'Well? And what do you say, boy? Do you want to learn chimney sweeping?'

Now Oliver had been told exactly what to say. Mr Bumble had warned him to smile and look happy 'or else'. But when the magistrate asked straight out like

---

[4] The passageways within a chimney.

that, face-to-face and with real kindness in his voice, the truth came spilling out of Oliver in a great jumble of terror: *'If-you-please-sir-send-me-back-to-the-workhouse-and-let-them-lock-me-up-and-let-them-beat-me-and-let-them-starve-me-and-let-me-die-but-**don't-make-me-go-up-the-chimneys!**'*

So Mr Gamfield did not get his five pounds or his boy, and Oliver went back to the workhouse, by order of the magistrate.

The Board of Governors decided then and there that Oliver was destined to join the Navy. After all, it is as good a place as any for a wicked boy to get himself hanged. So Oliver was one day away from a life on the high seas when a chance visitor changed his destiny.

Mr Sowerberry's work often brought him to the workhouse. He was an undertaker,[5] you see, and hungry, hopeless people have an obstinate habit of dying. Once or twice a week Mr Sowerberry would be summoned to measure up a bony body and carry it away for burial.

On this particular visit, Mr Bumble pointed out the poster on the door: **£5 Reward**. 'Would you perhaps be in need of a boy, Mr Sowerberry?' he asked.

And Mr Sowerberry replied, 'Do you know what, Mr Bumble? I believe I am.'

'Ah! This is the boy, is it?' said Mr Sowerberry, examining Oliver by the light of a wax-white candle when Mr Bumble delivered him to the undertaker's shop. 'He's very small.'

'He'll grow,' said Mr Bumble. 'He'll grow.'

'Don't I know it?' complained the undertaker's wife. 'He'll grow from eating our food!' She introduced Oliver to his supper (the dog's dinner) and his bed (under the shop counter). 'Don't mind sleeping among the coffins, do you brat?' she asked. 'Don't much matter if you do:

---

[5] Someone who organizes funerals.

there's nowhere else.'

So Oliver bedded down that night surrounded by teetering coffins. At every moment he expected a dead man to rise up out of one, howling and gibbering. Shutting his eyes, Oliver was almost envious of the Dead sleeping in the peaceful dark of their quiet graves.

CHAPTER 3

in which Oliver pays his respects to the Dead

Oliver was woken next morning by a frantic kicking at the undertaker's shop door. Hurrying to unlock it, he opened the door to a big, ugly, ragged boy. 'Did you want a coffin, sir?' he asked timidly.

'Don't know who I am, do you?' said Noah Claypole, banging him on the head and pushing past into the shop. 'You must be the new boy.'

All his life Noah Claypole had been teased and taunted by other boys who called him 'Noah Nobody', 'Mr Rags', and 'The Coffin Nail'. Now, finding a boy even more helpless than himself, Noah got his own back. Whenever Mr Sowerberry was out of the room, Noah Claypole would punch, kick, and jeer at Oliver.

But to Noah's fury and disgust, Oliver was a success. Mr Sowerberry gave him a tall black hat, a long black hat band, and had him lead the funeral processions of little children to the graveyard. The sight of this tiny, white-faced boy, tears glittering in his blue eyes, brought a gasp or a sigh from everyone who saw it, and business did very nicely. Thanks to an outbreak of measles, there was plenty of work, too, that autumn for little Oliver and his tall black hat. Once, after a particularly handsome funeral, Mr Sowerberry gave Oliver a penny and told him he had done well.

Enraged and jealous, Noah Claypole searched his small brain for some new way of tormenting Oliver.

'Twist? Twist? What kind of a name is that, then?' he began at suppertime. (They shared their daily ration of food: that is to say, Noah ate the meat and Oliver was left with the bones to suck.) 'Tell us about yerself. What's yer mother?'

'My mother's dead,' said Oliver with surprising heat. 'Don't talk about her!'

Noah knew at once what would hurt Oliver most. 'Just as well she's dead, ain't it, or she'd be hanged or locked up by now. I heard tell she was a thoroughly bad sort.'

'Don't you say anything against my mother!' said Oliver, overturning his bowl as he jumped to his feet.

Noah smirked and spread his hands. 'I was just saying. I'm very *sorry* for you – being born to a mother like that, what with her thieving and her drinking and her . . . *OW!*'

Oliver hurled himself across the table and, mustering all his strength, heaved a blow at Noah, then another and another and another.

'*Ow! Ow! Help! Get him off me! Oliver's killing me! Help!*' snivelled Noah, curling himself up into a ball on the kitchen floor as Oliver punched and pummelled him, yelling, 'Take that back! Take that back!'

The noise brought Mrs Sowerberry and the scullery maid[6] rushing in. They shrieked at the sight of little Oliver hammering away at the huge, lumpen Noah. 'Lor'! He's gone mad! The boy's gone mad! We'll all be murdered where we stand! Poor little Noah! Stop it, you murderous little villain!'

They tried to pull Oliver away, but he was lost in a red fog of rage and he struggled and lashed out and went on bellowing, '*Take it back! Take it back!*'

Somehow, the three of them scratched, slapped, and kicked Oliver until they could pull him upright. Then

---

[6] A humble kitchen servant.

they bundled him into the coalhole,[7] slammed the door, and shot the bolt. Oliver, still boiling with outrage, kicked at the coalhole door with both feet, and kept on kicking long after Noah had stopped whimpering. A sacred corner of Oliver's soul had been invaded and despite his cramped, choking prison, meek little Oliver Twist raged on behalf of his wronged mother.

When Mr Sowerberry came home, the bang-bang-banging was still loud in the kitchen, and Noah Claypole was still whining. Mr Bumble was sent for (because beadles know what to do with mad boys) and arrived puffing and blowing and wielding his long stick. 'It's *meat*, Mrs Sowerberry!' he declared. 'You have been feeding him *meat*, and this is what comes of it!'

Finally, Oliver was taken out of the coalhole, and knocked about like a whipping top[8] before being sent, bruised and bleeding, to his bed among the coffins. Only then did rage give way to sorrow. Only then did the full misery of his life grind down on him like a millstone. Only then did he allow himself to cry.

Oliver lay on his mattress under the shop counter and waited for night to crawl by. Before dawn, he got up, tied his few belongings into a bundle, and slipped out of the shop door. The street was silent. Never before had the winter stars seemed such a long way from the earth.

---

[7] A small cellar for storing coal.

[8] A toy set spinning with a string whip.

Hurrying as fast as his aching bones would let him, Oliver left town. Dodging from hedge to hedge, from ditch to ditch, he kept out of sight all morning, for fear they might come after him, hunting the runaway apprentice. Noon found him sitting on a milestone by the roadside, wondering, for the first time, where he was going.

He had just one penny, two pairs of socks, and a crust of bread. How far could a boy hope to get on those? Looking down at his stony seat, he read: LONDON 70 MILES. London! It was a place so far-off that even Mr Sowerberry and Mr Bumble had never been there. And yet everyone talked of London: huge and legendary and full of possibilities! A coach rattled by, but Oliver had no money for coaches. If he was going to go to London, he would have to walk every step of the way!

Oliver walked. He slept in haystacks. He begged water at cottage doors. He spent his penny on a loaf, but in a day it was gone. Hunger was his constant companion; it stuck close, like a big, loyal, vicious dog. But at the edge of every village, notices threatened him with arrest if he dared ask anyone for a bite to eat:

NO BEGGING
Beggars will be put in prison

Seventy miles! In muddy farmyards, farmers threatened to set the dogs on him. Passengers leaned out of stagecoach windows and teased him with coins . . . but never let the coins fall. Oliver thought he must surely drop down and die of hunger and exhaustion like his mother before him.

Villages gave way to towns – the towns that cluster round London like lambs around a sheep. In the market town of Barnet, Oliver sat down to rest on a doorstep, his cut feet clogged with bloody dust, his stomach empty. Passers-by stared, or stepped round him, but Oliver was too weary even to see them.

After a time, though, he became dimly aware of a boy on the other side of the road, watching him, sizing him up. Oliver closed his eyes.

'Watchya, my dear!' said a voice. 'What's doing?' The boy had crossed the street and was standing in front of Oliver now, his hands on his hips. He wore a man's coat, which reached down to his ankles, and he had folded the sleeves right back, to let his hands see daylight. There was a hat balanced on the very corner of his head; every time it threatened to slip off, the boy twitched it back into place with a jerk of his head. He had sharp, dark eyes and a grin like April Fool's Day. 'Pleased to meechya! How's things, my dear? Running away from the Law, is you? Ain't we all? Fancy a bite to eat and a glass of something warming? Dare say you're looking for somewhere to sleep tonight. I know just the place.' He reached out a hand. 'Jack Dawkins is the name, though there's some as call me the Artful Dodger.'

CHAPTER 4

in which Oliver meets Fagin and his wipe-swipers

Jack Dawkins led Oliver into the very heart of stony, treeless London. They passed huge churches, law courts and theatres, the oily, coiling River Thames, prisons, parks and palaces. Thousands of people, of every rank and profession hurried by, while dogs and beggars sprawled in doorways.

Broad avenues gave way to narrow alleyways full of tumbledown houses. Amid the worst slums of all, where the houses seemed on the very point of falling down, desperate figures lurked in the mud-dark shadows. The Artful Dodger stepped suddenly in at a doorway. He gave a low whistle, called a password then darted down some rickety stairs, dragging Oliver by the hand.

Tripping and stumbling, Oliver arrived in a big cellar. There, bent over a cooking pot like a witch over a cauldron, stood an old man. His rust-red hair burned like a flue above his dirty coat collar. When he turned round, his ugly face seemed to have been screwed in place with a hooked nose as big as the beak on a vulture. 'Ah! Dodger, my dear! Who is this you've brought with you?'

'This here is Oliver,' said the Artful Dodger. 'Oliver Twist. He's legging it from a master what didn't treat him with respect. Oliver, this is the kind, the generous Mister Fagin.' Oliver bowed.

The room stirred. From every corner and crevice, boys stood up, their faces bright with welcome.

'My name's Bates, Charlie Bates.'

'Just call me Kags. Everyone does.'

'And me, I'm flash Toby Crackitt!'

They crowded round Oliver, shaking his hand, offering to take his jacket, even reaching into his pockets in case he was carrying something uncomfortably heavy. They were ragged, grubby boys, but their eyes had a shine Oliver had never seen in the workhouse.

Mesmerized by the smell of sausages cooking, Oliver gazed around him. A rack of silk handkerchiefs fluttered in the draught, like a ship dressed all over in flags.

'Wipes,' explained the old gentleman, following Oliver's gaze. 'We have just looked them out for washing. Haven't we, boys? . . . But let's hear how hard my boys have worked today . . . Dodger, what did you make?'

'Two wallets,' said Jack Dawkins.

'Lined?'

'See for yourself.' The Artful Dodger pulled out the wallets from the deep pockets of his coat. Oliver was astounded that the Artful Dodger should be able to 'make' something so fine.

'And you, Kags?' said Fagin.

'Wipes,' said Kags, and pulled out two silk handkerchiefs.

Fagin inspected the work closely. 'Good, good. But these initials embroidered here – they'll have to be unpicked.' (Oliver was amazed. Fancy a boy being able to embroider silk so delicately!) 'How would you like to make such things, my dear?' Fagin enquired, turning to Oliver.

'I'd like that very much indeed, sir!' answered Oliver. He could not understand why Charlie Bates began to hoot with laughter.

Fagin and his boys played a quaint game that night. Fagin, decked out with a pocket watch, a cravat pin, two wallets, a purse, and four or five handkerchiefs minced or strode or waddled or tiptoed or limped about the room in such a comical way that Oliver laughed 'til he wept. Meanwhile, the brotherhood of boys tried to take things from Fagin without being spotted. Whenever they did, the old man praised them as warmly as any father. Could it be that this cheery, tender-hearted old fellow looked after this whole swarm of scruffy boys? No wonder, then, that he had nothing left to spend on clothes or home comforts for himself!

With a meal of sausages inside him, Oliver fell asleep as soon as he was shown a bed to sleep in. Next day, the other boys rose and went out about their day's business, but Oliver slept on. Even when he woke, he did not stir at once. It was pleasant to float between waking and sleeping. He was aware of the old man scraping a saucepan with a spoon, moving about the room, bending to lift something heavy. Oliver finally parted his eyelids.

Fagin was peering into a small oak box, leering with pleasure. Dipping in two bony fingers, he plucked up a gold watch studded with gems. There were six more like it. There were rings and necklaces, bracelets, and brooches, too. There were things so fancy that Oliver could not even give them a name, but their sparkle made the old man's eyes glitter. Oliver knew this because the eyes were looking directly at him.

Clack! The box lid shut. 'Awake? What's your game? Why aren't you asleep? Snooping, were you? Did you see?' Fagin picked up a bread knife and lunged across the room towards Oliver.

'P-please, sir, I couldn't sleep any more!'

'Did you see them? Did you see my pretties?' The bread knife trembled almost as much as Oliver.

'Y-yes, sir!' said Oliver who never told a lie.

'They're mine, see!' declared the old man. 'Savings! Comfort for my old age! Understand?'

Oliver nodded dumbly, his blue eyes round and innocent.

Suddenly Fagin put down the knife, snickering nervously. 'Just you fetch over that bucket of water, will you young Oliver?' And by the time Oliver had returned with the bucket, the oak treasure box was gone, returned in a twinkling to its hiding place.

'How would you like to learn a trade, Oliver my dear?' said Fagin, oozing friendliness once again. 'The one those other boys were learning last night?' He poked a handkerchief into the breast pocket of his shabby coat.

All Oliver had to do was to pull it out without Fagin feeling it go.

They practised this game many times in the following weeks, until Oliver was so clever at it that Fagin called him 'a most promising young gentleman' . . . and yet still he was kept indoors. When the other boys went off to work in the mornings, Oliver stayed shut up in the apartment, unpicking embroidered initials or practising 'Where's-the-Wallet?' with Fagin. When his boys came home, and Fagin asked to see what they had 'made' during the day, they showed him all manner of valuable things. The best always came from the Artful Dodger. 'Model yourself on this boy,' Fagin told Oliver, throwing an affectionate arm around the Artful Dodger. 'Make him your model, my dear! He will go a long way – a long, long way.'

There were visitors, too. A jolly, giggling girl with a red frock and cheeks to match came with messages for Fagin. Her name was Nancy, and Fagin's boys adored her pretty face and laughing ways – especially Charlie Bates, who was utterly love-sick. Sometimes Nancy's sweetheart came too, to talk business with Fagin: a man called Bill Sikes, whose temper made Fagin look positively loving. Sikes growled more fiercely than the dog that skulked along behind him, and he smelled of drink and sweat and blood.

At last, after several weeks, Oliver was allowed to make his first trip out-of-doors. Fagin put him in the care of the Artful Dodger and Charlie Bates, and waved them goodbye from the top of the rotten, crumbling stairs.

The Artful Dodger and Charlie Bates did not seem in any great hurry to get to work. They strolled along, hands in pockets, reading notices, and looking in shop windows. Oliver strolled with them, wondering whether he would spend the day stitching wallets or embroidering wipes.

Suddenly the Artful Dodger's manner changed – like a dog that sees a rabbit. They were passing a bookstall, where a wealthy, white-haired gentleman stood browsing through the books on sale. The Artful Dodger crossed the road and stood just behind the old gentleman. Perhaps, thought Oliver, he was trying to read the book over his shoulder . . . Then a hand shot out and back.

One moment a handkerchief lapped out of the gentleman's coat pocket; the next it was gone, crumpled into the Artful Dodger's fist until he turned and passed it to Charlie. Both boys set off running.

The whole thing took seconds. Inside those seconds Oliver understood everything. He understood how Fagin and his band of boys lived, and why they practised long and hard. He understood the oak chest hidden under the

floor and the seven watches inside it. He also understood that he was a party to the crime.

Feeling inside his pocket, Mr Brownlow found his handkerchief gone and spun round, hoping to spot the thief. He saw a young, fair-haired boy, his face a picture of guilt, turn and start to run for all he was worth.

'*Stop! Thief!*' called Mr Brownlow, and then louder, **'STOP! THIEF!'**

CHAPTER 5

in which Oliver answers for his crimes

There is something magical about the words, 'Stop! Thief!' They have the power to start everyone running – the butcher, the schoolboy, the postman, and the housemaid. People drop whatever they are doing and join in the chase. Louder and louder it sounds, *'Stop! Thief!* **Stop! Thief!***'* Even Charlie Bates and the Artful Dodger joined in (though that was only to keep suspicion from falling on them.)

Mr Brownlow was not so fast on his feet as some, and it was another man who finally caught up with Oliver Twist and felled him with one almighty punch. By the time Mr Brownlow arrived, Oliver lay, stunned and bleeding, on the ground. Such a very *little* boy. And his face ... there was something about his face, which set Mr Brownlow's memory flickering like a lantern slide show. Where had he seen that face before? A police officer arrived and wanted details.

'My pocket was picked. I thought that this boy ... ' began Mr Brownlow. At once the policeman collared Oliver and dragged him to his feet. 'Gently, please!' Mr Brownlow remonstrated. 'I am by no means sure ... '

But the wheels of the Law had started to turn, and Oliver was caught in their cogs. He was searched, of course. No handkerchief was found, but what did that prove? He could have passed it to an accomplice. He was dragged away to the Magistrates' Court, where it so happened the renowned magistrate Fang was sitting in judgement.

Magistrate Fang had been drinking port since breakfast and was in the mood to dispense Justice.

'Look here, sir, I am not at all sure that I wish this trial to go ahead . . . ' Mr Brownlow felt things were getting out of hand.

'Who is this villain? Wassee done?' demanded the judge.

The court usher tried to smooth out the mistake. 'He's done nothing, m'lord. This gentleman is the one who was robbed.'

'The boy's clearly not well!' protested Mr Brownlow. 'See how pale he is! He can barely stand!'

'Whoever he ish, he'sh annoying me,' slurred the judge.

'I must protest!' cried Mr Brownlow. 'What kind of justice is this? I say I could have been mistaken! There was nothing found on the boy!'

But magistrate Fang had his own ideas. 'I find the boy guilty. Six months in prison . . . '

'This is an outrage!' cried Mr Brownlow.

'. . . with hard labour. Take him down.'

'Wait!' The door of the courtroom burst open and in ran the owner of the bookstall. 'I saw everything!' he cried.

'Too late,' said the judge. 'Trial's over.'

'I had to find someone to mind my stall or I would have come before,' explained the bookseller. 'But I saw it all! That boy in the dock didn't do it. It was two others . . . By the way, sir, you still have my book.'

Mr Brownlow looked down at the novel grasped tightly in his hand. 'Bless me, so I do!'

'Aha! Knew he was a rogue!' slurred the judge vengefully.

Much against his nature, Magistrate Fang was obliged to let Oliver go.

Oliver, however, knew none of this. White as a new-born lamb, and quaking with fever, he had already slumped sideways in the dock and was lying there, as still as death. He was still unconscious when the constable threw him out into the street.

Mr Brownlow, appalled, went and crouched beside the boy. 'There now, child. You are coming home with me. It is the very least I can do.'

At the back of the jostling crowd, Charlie Bates and the Artful Dodger glanced at one another. Then they melted away into the city hubbub.

CHAPTER 6

in which Oliver meets with kindness

Sitting by the stove, warming a tankard of ale, Fagin heard a low whistle, then footsteps on the stairs. Strange? Only two pairs of feet? Where was the third? By the time Charlie and the Artful Dodger reached the doorway, Fagin was ready with a curse to throw at them. 'Where's Oliver? What's happened to the boy?' he demanded.

'Nabbed,' said the Artful Dodger.

'Nabbed and let off and took home by the same man as got robbed!' said Charlie, still laughing at the events of the day.

The Artful Dodger knew better than to laugh. 'Oliver won't snitch on us,' he said uncertainly. 'We're his mates.'

'Fool!' In his rage and panic, Fagin threw the tankard of ale. Dodger ducked and the tankard flew through the doorway and struck the wall, spilling its contents over someone on the stairs. A head appeared, spitting and cursing, and there stood Bill Sikes, like a black squall, his three-day beard dripping ale, his dirty red neckerchief soaked. Behind him, the claws of his surly little dog scrabbled on the floor.

'Who won't snitch?' demanded Bill Sikes, and the very beams of the attic quaked with terror.

Day after day Oliver lay unconscious. For a whole week he knew nothing of the spotless bed he lay in, the elegant bedroom, the comfortable house to which Mr Brownlow had brought him. The sheets were soft and white; the room was warm and quiet. A doctor came and went, but Oliver, buried beneath illness and fatigue, knew nothing of it. It was as if he had to worm his way upwards through all the years of weariness and fear, hunger and cruelty.

When he first woke, a woman sat at the end of the bed. Bewildered, he watched her through his eyelashes. When she saw his eyelids flicker, however, Mrs Bedwin did not come at him with a bread knife or curse or pounce. She simply burst into tears of joy. 'Bless you! Awake at last! We were so worried! Wait 'til I tell the Master!'

There was broth to eat – and more for the asking. There was warm water to wash in; there were clean nightshirts to wear. When he was stronger, Oliver learned to play cribbage[9] with Mrs Bedwin, the housekeeper.

---

[9] A game of cards.

At last Mr Brownlow sent for him, and Oliver was taken down to the library – a room lined from floor to ceiling with all manner and sizes of rich-smelling books. Oliver gazed around him, noting everything in the room: the shine of polished wood, the slow drip-drop of the clock, the fresh flowers in a vase, the pictures on the wall. One picture in particular held his eye. It was of a young woman, pale and pretty, with a small face, large eyes, and a coronet of golden hair. For some reason it made Oliver's heart pound; his eyes fill with tears.

'Whatever is the matter, boy?' asked Mr Brownlow in distress. 'There, there now. Let's get you back to bed.'

'That picture!' said Oliver. 'The lady has such a sweet face!' His cheeks grew hot; his head swam.

The next time Oliver entered the library, he looked at once for the picture of the lady . . . but it was gone.

'The Master feared it upset you in some way,' said Mrs Bedwin.

'Oh no! No, it didn't! It made me very, very happy!'

'Then you must get fit and well,' said Mrs Bedwin, stroking his hair, 'and the picture shall be hung up again.'

The matter of the picture seemed to prey on Mr Brownlow's mind. He spent a lot of time brooding about times long gone, and became quiet, almost sad. He asked Oliver to recount his whole life's history, and listened, with patience and sympathy, while Oliver told it.

Finally the old gentleman confided sadly in Oliver, 'I have put my trust in people before now and been betrayed. Never let me down, Oliver Twist; I do not think my old heart could bear it.'

'I never would!' vowed Oliver. 'Not ever!'

'Find him, my dears!' said Fagin, meanwhile, to his army of boys. 'Seek him up and down, in and out! Dodge about, Dodger! Use your eyes and ears, but find little Oliver, and find him fast!'

'Yeah, find him, Fagin, you mangy old dog,' snarled Bill Sikes. 'Find him before he spills what he knows. That boy could put your head into a noose if he snitched.'

'And your head, too, my dear,' whispered the old man, with an oily, uneasy smile, 'And yours. Because if I go down, we both go down together, you and I.'

CHAPTER 7

in which Oliver is put to the test

Those quiet days at Mr Brownlow's house in Pentonville were the happiest Oliver had ever known. His whole life had been lived out to the noise of spoons scraping on tin, of shouts and kicks and blows, of quarrels and cursing. Now, peace muffled every step, every closing door, every mealtime and every night's sleep. Oliver quickly came to love Mr Brownlow, Mrs Bedwin, and the faces which looked down at him from portraits on the wall. It seemed, too, that he was loved in return . . . by all but one.

Mr Brownlow had a lifelong friend called Mr Grimwig – an argumentative gentleman with a large, powdered wig and a walking stick that he rapped sternly against floor or table whenever he offered his opinion. Mr Grimwig had a great many opinions, and he held them very strongly. In fact Mr Grimwig always took the opposite point of view for the joy of it. Yet somehow his pigheadedness never marred the friendship. He and Mr Brownlow were friends, and true friends do not have to agree on everything.

'That boy is not to be trusted,' said Mr Grimwig of

Oliver. 'As soon as he is fit, he will go back to a life of crime. He will, or I'll eat my head!'

'Never,' said Mr Brownlow, equably. 'Life has treated him with great cruelty, but he is a good boy at heart.'

'You are too kind, Brownlow; too kind and too trusting! The boy will take advantage of you. He will, or I'll eat my head!'

One day, Mrs Bedwin burst into Oliver's room brandishing a hairbrush, her face flushed with excitement. 'Mr Brownlow has sent for you,' she said. 'Let me make you look presentable.'

So Oliver put on his new suit and went downstairs to where Mr Brownlow and Mr Grimwig sat eating muffins. When Oliver entered, Mr Brownlow looked so sombre and serious that Oliver was suddenly afraid.

'Oliver, I mean to send you . . . '

'Oh please, sir! Don't sent me away!' Oliver burst out. 'Take back this suit. Let me work as a servant, but don't send me back out on the streets!'

'Calm yourself, boy. I was simply going to ask if you would like to run an errand for me.'

'Oh! I'd like that very much!' said Oliver, who had been cooped up in the house for six long weeks.

'These books must be returned to the bookseller. And here are the five pounds I owe him.'

Proudly Oliver took the pile of books and tucked the

crinkling white bank note into his pocket. He had never handled so much money in all his life. Mr Grimwig watched, rocking his big head to and fro, scowling disapproval and tapping his cane on the floor. Oliver bowed to him politely and headed for the door.

'Come straight back,' said Mr Brownlow.

'Oh, I will, sir!' promised Oliver.

Pausing on the tall stone steps of the house, dazzled by the winter sunshine, Oliver looked both ways along the empty street then set off eagerly on his mission.

'And that is the last you will see of him,' said Mr

Grimwig, helping himself to a muffin. 'He has five pounds and a pile of valuable books. Even now he is running back to his robbers' den, laughing at you every step of the way. He is, or I'll eat my . . . '

'Nonsense!' said Mr Brownlow. 'He will be back inside twenty minutes.'

The big clock in the corner counted each passing second. 'Half an hour at most,' said Mr Brownlow.

The light faded in the window, but still the two friends sat, the lamp unlit, while the clock's hands passed slowly over its stark, white face.

Oliver stopped for a moment to get his bearings. The bookshop must be around the next turning on the left . . . A young woman in a bonnet and carrying a little basket was crossing the street. She quickened her pace, until she was running towards him. Her arms engulfed Oliver, her skirts washed round his legs. His face was pressed to her chest. For a moment he could not breathe.

'Oh there you are, you naughty boy! I've found you at last! How could you run off like that and drive us all mad with worry?'

'Nancy?' Oliver struggled to break free, but Nancy was holding him too tightly.

People noticing the struggle saw a tearful girl clasping

close a long-lost little brother. 'He ran off last week and we've been searching for him day and night!' she explained in a shrill wail. 'Oh come home with me, little brother, before our poor mother dies of a broken heart!'

'No! It's not true! Help me!' gasped Oliver, but the passers-by only shook their heads reproachfully at him and smiled at his kidnapper.

The precious books dropped to the pavement. Out of a side alley stepped a third person to pick them up. There was a dirty red bandanna around his throat, a white dog at his heels. Bill Sikes took hold of Oliver's other wrist so tightly that he thought it would break, and together Nancy and Sikes forced Oliver down the alley where no one would see what became of him.

'Bullseye!' hissed Sikes at the dog. 'Watch 'im!' And he pointed to Oliver's throat. 'Now if you run, boy, the dog will rip you in pieces.'

Seeing that there was no escape, Oliver stopped struggling.

CHAPTER 8

in which things look black for Oliver

'Did you nark on us?' snarled Bill Sikes, pushing his scarred head close to Oliver's. 'Did you go gabbing to your high-and-mighty friends about us?'

'No, sir! Truly!' gasped Oliver, gibbering with terror.

''Cause if you did, I'll fix it so you never speak another word to nobody never! Understand?' Oliver nodded dumbly then, as Sikes wrenched on his arm, broke into a trot to keep up. His kidnappers hustled him away to the darker side of London Town.

They were given a noisy welcome on his return to Fagin's den of thieves. The boys crowded round Oliver, laughing and pointing.

'Look at Oliver!'

'Look at them shoes!'

'Woah! Fancy books!'

'Ain't he the little toff?'

'Shame to spoil that nice new suit, ain't it Mr Fagin?'

Fagin's leering face swept close to Oliver's face. 'Quite right, my dears. Better change back into your working clothes, Oliver.'

As soon as Oliver saw his old suit hanging from a nail,

he realized how they had tracked him down. Mrs Bedwin, in presenting him with his new suit, had given the old one to a rag-and-bone man at the door. The suit, like some small, greasy, stolen boy, had passed from one pair of dishonest hands into another and another, until at last they came to Fagin, who carefully unravelled their secrets.

The Artful Dodger dipped deep into Oliver's pocket and fetched out the five-pound note. Fagin snatched it, saying, 'It's mine! The books you can keep, all right Bill?'

'Hand it over, you old rogue,' said Sikes, drawing a knife. 'We earned it, Nancy and I. You sell the books if you can find someone to buy 'em.'

'Oh no! Please! Give them back!' cried Oliver in desperation. 'You must send them back to Mr Brownlow! Keep me, but send back the money and the books – or he'll think I robbed him!'

The two men's eyes fell on him: in the heat of the quarrel he had almost slipped their mind. 'So he will, my dear. So he will,' mused Fagin, and a hideous grin slowly split his face. 'How very well things are turning out.'

In spite of her part in recapturing Oliver, Nancy seemed the only one with any pity for his plight. 'Lord forgive me, what have I done?' she whispered. She was very pale and her eyes were very bright. 'I've robbed for you, Fagin, since I was younger than Oliver here. I've done whatever I had to do to survive. I'm nobody and nothing and there's no help for me. But him? He had a chance! Oliver had a chance to lead a decent life. Now what's in store for him except to cheat and steal and blacken his soul working for you, you old devil. He'll end up rotting in prison or swinging from a rope, while you squirrel up the loot!' She was raging now, tearing at her hair and clothes. The brotherhood of boys gaped at her, unnerved, afraid.

'Do something, Bill!' hissed the old man. 'Her noise will fetch in the Law!'

'Oh I can shut her up soon enough,' said Sikes uneasily. 'Sometimes she gets like this, but it don't last. That's the thing with women. Nothing lasts long with them.' He 'fixed' Nancy with a slap that knocked her down. The watching boys flinched. For a moment their cheery, raucous little world was shown in its true light: fear and violence, dog-eat-dog.

Oliver looked to the door, but the dog Bullseye growled and wriggled closer, fixing its bloodshot eyes on Oliver's throat.

Long after dark the two friends still sat, listening to the tick of the clock, hoping to hear Oliver's feet on the front steps. Long after all hope had passed, they went on waiting. Even Mr Grimwig, who had won the bet, wished he had not.

'Perhaps he got lost – or was set upon and robbed,' said Mr Brownlow.

'Perhaps he did,' said Mr Grimwig. 'You should offer a reward for any information.'

Mr Brownlow brightened a little. 'I shall do that! I shall put a notice in the newspaper tomorrow morning!'

Then they sat on in the darkness, each lost in their own thoughts, each returning time and time again to the thought of Oliver Twist.

◆◆◆

Mr Bumble the Beadle glanced idly through the newspaper as he sat waiting for a train. He was on his way to Birmingham on parochial[10] business. His eyes fell on an advertisement in large black type:

> # FIVE GUINEA REWARD
>
> to any person having information
> concerning one OLIVER TWIST
> or how he may be found

The familiar name twisted itself into Mr Bumble's heart like a corkscrew.

At once, Mr Bumble altered his travel plans and caught the next train to London. By evening he was in Pentonville.

'Oh I knew there would be news of him! I knew it!' declared Mrs Bedwin, hurrying him into the house. 'Bless his heart! I said so all along!'

Mr Bumble was ushered into the parlour, where Mr Brownlow and Mr Grimwig showered him with

---

[10] To do with the parish; the area a parish council looks after.

questions. Mr Bumble's chest swelled with self-importance. He laid his tricorn hat on the table and perched, very upright, on the edge of his chair. 'I know the boy's history from the day of his birth until he deserted his duties and ran off to London, and every minute of it was filled with villainy and deceit, sir!' Then settling himself like a chicken on to her eggs, the Beadle began to tell the story he was sure Mr Brownlow wanted to hear.

It was a story of a thieving, lazy, spiteful boy, born of vicious, common parents; a boy who would rather brawl and cheat than do an honest day's work. It was the story of a sly boy who used his innocent good looks to worm his way into kindly hearts only to trick and deceive them. 'In short, there never was such an ungrateful, dishonest, peevish, unpleasant child in the history of the world!' declared Mr Bumble, folding his hands around his staff of office and smiling grimly.

For a long time, Mr Brownlow did not speak or stir. Then he counted out five golden guineas into the Beadle's hand. 'I am grateful to you, sir. The reward is yours . . . though I would gladly have paid you three times as much to hear you speak well of the boy.'

'Oh!' said Mr Bumble, wishing he had known this before. Sadly it was too late to unsay the lies he had just told.

CHAPTER 9

in which the robbery takes place

How to bind him to a life of crime? That was the problem that plagued old Fagin night and day. Oliver's honest nature was proving too hard to break, and yet someone would not be pleased to hear that. Not pleased at all . . .

Bill Sikes was in favour of cutting the boy's throat – shutting his mouth once and for all; luckily Nancy had talked him out of that. But how to bind Oliver, body and soul, to a life of crime? That was the question.

The answer came to Fagin one night, as he shared a bottle of gin with the house-breaker Sikes. 'Have you done that little job you was talking about, Bill my dear?' asked Fagin, eyes glittering in the candlelight. 'The one you and young Toby Crackitt planned? The one in Chertsey?'

'There's a snag,' snarled Sikes. 'I've looked it over. But the way in is too small. We need a boy. Toby's grown far too big.'

'A boy?'

'A boy. Small as possible. I'd use Ned the Sweep but

he was nabbed last month and now he's walking the treadmill in Newgate prison.'

Fagin strummed the end of his long, beaky nose. 'A boy, eh?'

'Better be trustworthy, or I'll have your guts for it, old man.'

'Well, now I think of it . . . I believe I shall loan you . . . Oliver.'

'Oliver?!'

'Think on it, Bill my dear. Once he's worked with you, there's no going back for him. Once he's . . . helped you out, Oliver will be one of us!'

Bill Sikes turned this idea over like a stolen pocket watch, looking at it from all sides. 'He'd best not make trouble or I'll blow his brains out!'

Fagin hushed him like a baby. 'Bill, Bill, my dear. Would I give you bad advice? You are my friend! My bread and butter! I depend on your success. Speak lower, though, or your woman will hear us.'

Seated by the hearth, however, Nancy sat gazing vacantly into the fire. She seemed to pay the men at the table no attention at all. 'I'll send her to fetch him, night after next,' said Bill, and gulped down another glass of gin. When at last Sikes sank to the floor in a drunken stupor, Fagin got up, gave him a sly kick, and let himself out onto the wintry streets.

Oliver was alone when Nancy came to get him. Fagin had gone out to keep an appointment with a man called Monks, locking the door, leaving the boy with a lit candle and a book to read. Oliver knew that he was to be loaned to Bill Sikes, but could not imagine why. Then a key turned in the door's lock.

'Come child. It's time to go. You mustn't keep Bill waiting.'

A kind of hope stirred in Oliver at the sight of Nancy's bruised and weary face. The moment they were in the street, he would break free and call for help. Kind-hearted Nancy would not stop him. Yes! He would shout out the truth until somebody listened and believed him.

Nancy was a clever girl. She could read a face as other people read books. She knew at once what Oliver was thinking. 'Listen here, Oliver. I've spoken out for you – and I will again – but Bill always makes me suffer for it, after. I'll help you one day, but today ain't the time. If I don't take you directly to him now – and quick – he'll kill me for sure. So be a good boy, Oliver, and come with me.'

Oliver's last hopes blew out along with the candle. He put his hand into Nancy's and allowed himself to be led downstairs to a waiting horse-cab.

For two whole days Sikes and Oliver toiled on foot, westwards – clear across London and out into a raw, sodden countryside. At last they came to a place so desolate and lonely that Oliver thought the burglar must mean to murder and bury him here where no one would ever find the body. At the end of a lane, however, Sikes let himself into a ramshackle hut. A familiar face greeted them out of the shadows. Toby Crackitt was already there, waiting, and the two thieves settled to an evening of drinking while Oliver slept, exhausted by the long, cold, dismal journey.

It was the dead of night when they roused him. A cold walk, a garden wall, a big dark house with shutters at every window. Sikes put a crowbar to a small, high shutter and prised it open. 'Now, boy. When you get inside, go directly to the front door and unbolt it. Let us in . . . and not a sound, you hear, or I'll skin you.'

'Oh no, sir! Not robbery!' Oliver fell on his knees in the mud and lifted up his hands, pleading. 'Don't make me do it! Don't make me!'

Bill Sikes drew a pistol from his pocket and pressed the muzzle against Oliver's forehead. His finger tightened on the trigger. 'I warned you . . .'

'Do you want to wake the house, you fool?' hissed Toby, knocking the pistol aside. 'A knife's quieter, if we must . . . Hush! What's that noise?'

Sikes swore silently. 'I didn't hear nothin'.'

The next moment Oliver was lifted up and posted,

feet-first, through the tiny window. Sikes lowered him to
the floor by the collar of his jacket. He found himself in
the scullery of the silent, sleeping house. 'Do it, brat,'
urged Sikes in a menacing whisper. 'I've got you in my
sights every step of the way.'

The moment Sikes took his hand from Oliver's collar,
Oliver started forward across the scullery and into the
hall. The street door was on his left, the staircase ahead
of him. Through the window behind him poked the
barrel of the pistol.

Dizzy with terror, Oliver felt the knowledge settle in

his stomach like vinegar. He would run up the stairs and try to rouse someone – try to warn them – try to save their belongings and to save his own soul from the sin of thieving.

'*Stop! Come back!*' It was Sikes. Had he read Oliver's thoughts? No. He had heard the turn of a door handle, the thud of feet on the landing above. Now the shouts came – a pair of faces, bleary and white – the barrel of a shotgun. Oliver froze, unable to move, unable to cry out. There was a powder flash, a massive explosion, and a blow, which threw Oliver backward against the wall. He heard Sikes bark out, '*Run for it, Toby! They've shot the brat!*'

CHAPTER 10

in which two of our characters lie at death's door

Oliver reeled back into the scullery and fell against the wall directly beneath the little scullery window. A hand took hold of his collar, and he was lifted up and backwards – dragged bodily through the window – and slung across Sikes' back. The two thieves ran back across the lawn, bundled their burden over the garden wall, and kept on running into the night, lugging Oliver along like a sack of loot. Forced to stop and catch his breath, Sikes cursed the figures that came on in hot pursuit. 'How the child bleeds!' he said in disgust.

'They're gaining on us!' yelled Toby. 'There's dogs, 'n' all! Let's split up! Leave the boy, Bill, and save yourself!' So laying Oliver down in a ditch and throwing his old brown cape over the body to hide it, Bill Sikes plunged away, leaping over a farm wall as he went and cursing like all the devils in Hell.

The butler and the under-butler from the big house both outran their courage at about the same time. It is wonderful how rage can make heroes out of the most ordinary people, but in the end, their bravery washed off in the rain, and both men were secretly glad to break off the chase and turn back for the house.

An icy rain was teeming, rattling on the muddy cape, but Oliver did not hear it. A chill worse than winter had crept into his limbs; a blackness darker than the night had enveloped him.

Oliver was woken by the sound of his own groans. He knew that if he did not stand up and move, he would die. Somehow he dragged himself out of the ditch and stumbled blindly on through hedges and across fields, until he glimpsed the lights of a house. As he crawled closer he realized, with dread and despair, that he had come full circle – to the very house where he had been shot. Too late to look elsewhere for help. Tugging on the bell-pull, Oliver sank down in the porch, more dead than alive. Voices washed over him – 'That's 'im! That's one of them!'

'Get him inside!'

'Call the police!'

'Call the mistress!'

'Call a doctor, or he's done for!'

'It's only a child. No more than a boy!'

'Fetch the police anyway! He's one of the thieves!'

The entire household filed into the bedroom, Miss Rose Maylie, her aunt, her butler and under-butler, and the parlour maids. The doctor, wearing his most serious face asked, 'Are you quite sure, Miss Maylie, that you are ready to view this desperado? He is not so very fierce just now, it's true, and I don't believe he will frighten you too gravely.'

'I am ready, Doctor,' said the young lady nervously.

The curtain was drawn back to reveal – Oliver asleep. His head rested on his arm, cheeks flushed with fever, and his long golden hair streamed across the pillow. The doctor's eyes twinkled with amusement.

'Oh, what are we going to do?' cried Miss Maylie. 'How could there be any wickedness in this poor child! Perhaps he was forced into helping the burglars! Or even if he wasn't, what do we know of the sufferings that drove him to it? How do we know what kind of loveless, miserable life he has led, with no one to love him or teach him right from wrong? Oh, we can't give him over to the police, Aunt. We can't!' And she burst into tears.

'Well, of course we shan't, my dear!' exclaimed her aunt. In fact everyone was agreed, so that when the police arrived, they found no one to arrest. 'A mistake, officers. We were too hasty in calling you. A boy,

officers? What boy? No boys here. So sorry to have troubled you. Let us show you to the door.'

When Oliver woke, he found himself in Paradise or somewhere very like it. The house was set in gardens, the garden in countryside, and the countryside in a softly curving corner of England as fresh and pretty as a painting with the paint still wet. The loudest noise was birdsong or the piano where Rose Maylie played and sang. The smells were of new-mown grass, wild flowers, blossom, and country cooking.

Oliver was treated with such kindness that he might have been a returning hero rather than a burglar's boy. He tried to repay that kindness by getting up early each day, by fetching and carrying, and by using his very best manners. But the harder he tried, the more loving the old woman and her niece became towards him, so that in the end he thought he might live to one hundred and never be able to repay their generosity.

They listened to his life history and, though thousands would have called him a liar, believed every word. They found him a teacher to help him with reading and writing, and pretty soon Oliver was able to read from the Bible each evening to Rose Maylie and her aunt – which made him as proud as the greatest preacher in the land.

Far away, in the workhouse where Oliver had once lived, a very old woman sat bolt upright in the bed and screamed, 'I am dying. I must tell someone what I did! Fetch the Matron. I must tell her.'

Mr Bumble had never realized before how many teaspoons Mrs Corney owned. He was very taken with her furniture, too. Mrs Corney had been called away to the bedside of a dying woman – one of the paupers in her charge. Left alone in the parlour, the Beadle took the opportunity to admire everything in the room. As Matron of the Workhouse, Mrs Corney lived rent-free he supposed. A widow with thirty teaspoons, eh, and living rent-free? A bachelor might do worse. In fact it was enough to put Mr Bumble into a highly romantic mood . . .

The lady herself was not best pleased to be called to a deathbed just when she was serving tea to a dashing gentleman caller. She muttered, climbing the draughty stairs, 'People ought to get on and die without disturbing their betters.'

This particular dying pauper was a midwife: at least she had helped many babies into the world during her years in the workhouse. At the sight of Mrs Corney, she heaved herself up off the pillow and began to confess, 'I should never have done it, Matron! She was cold and hungry, poor child, but still she hadn't sold it. Through all her hardships, she kept it around her neck until the day she died. She whispered to me, as she lay dying, "Give it to the child and tell him to pray for me – to forgive me . . . " But it was gold, wasn't it? And she was dead, and I was tempted. I took it and never let on. But it preyed on my conscience, it did. It preys on my conscience still. It was this bed – this very bed where she died – and now I'm adying. God forgive me! I must make amends. I must. Find the child. Give it to the child. Give it to little Oliver Twist!' The breath caught in her throat. The old woman fell back against the pillows . . . and Mrs Corney went back downstairs to her visitor, clutching the delicious secret to her breast.

in which new friends and old enemies appear

It was not such a great coincidence that Fagin and Monks should meet all those months ago. The Crooked Arms was the greatest haunt in all London for thieves, thugs, and villains. Stolen property changed hands there. Dirty deals were agreed there. Weapons were loaded, and plots hatched, booty picked over, and bribes paid. Both men and women got drunk, and fights broke out, while the innkeeper just watched and listened and smiled and poured pints and held his peace.

For a year now, Fagin and Monks had shared a secret, and that secret concerned Oliver.

'He had better not be dead! I never wanted him dead!' Monks was saying. 'Ruined, but not dead! All along I said . . . '

'All may be well my dear,' Fagin soothed him. 'All may still be well. There is nothing in the papers about a body.'

'You mean he may be alive?' gasped Monks. 'Worse and worse!' In the candlelight, his scarred face worked itself into grotesque grimaces. A vivid red scar on his neck burned hotly. 'Worse and worse!'

'Now now, my dear. There is no point in starting at shadows. Let us take a little jaunt, eh? A jaunt in the countryside. It would do us both good to breathe a little country air for a few weeks . . . '

There was a chilly draught, and a stronger smell of drains trickled in. Fagin's eyes darted to the opening door. 'Why, Nancy, my dear! Where have you been keeping yourself? How is my dear friend Mr Sikes?'

The girl was white-faced and weary. 'Not good, Fagin. Cold and wet he was after that . . . night out. Caught a fever. I've sat up with him day and night. When he wakes, he won't eat – only drink. Sent me here for beer. We're fearful low on cash, Fagin.' She eyed Monks. 'Any news of little Oliver?'

'What? No, none at all, my dear, but you know what they say: no news is good news. We all miss him. I cannot wait to have him back by my side, and that's the truth.'

Weeks slipped by. Spring gave way to summer and Oliver's soul unfurled like one of the cornfield poppies. Only one thought troubled his peaceful days: that of Mr Brownlow. 'He was so good to me. If only I could explain how things were. He must think that I stole his books and money. Perhaps he even hates me!'

'Hush Oliver. When you are quite well again, we shall go to London and find your Mr Brownlow, and no one in the world shall think badly of you.'

'Oh may we?' cried Oliver 'How wonderful it would be to see the dear, kind gentleman again! Oh thank you, Miss Rose! Thank you! Thank you!'

With such prospects in mind, Oliver could not settle to his reading book that day. There was birdsong. It was hot. The sun shone in through the window making the pages too bright. Oliver closed his eyes and dozed.

It was the kind of doze so shallow that he could still hear the birds, the church bell chiming, the poppy-heads popping and letting fall their seeds . . . He heard voices outside and the sunlight no longer fell on his face, but Oliver was too much asleep to open his eyes. In fact he knew he must be dreaming because all at once he was in London again, in Fagin's kitchen, hearing Fagin's voice . . .

'Is that him, my dear?'

'By all that stinks and rots and bleeds, it must be! It has to be! It is! He is the image of his wretched mother!'

'Calm yourself, my dear, or your illness will come upon you. It would not do. Not here. Not now. Come away.'

Oliver's blood ran cold. His eyes opened and there, within touching distance, was Fagin's beaky, sallow face, his shock of rust-red hair. Beside him stood a young man, his scarred face as white and crumpled as dirty

paper; foam spattering his lips. Oliver gave a shriek . . .
and the faces were gone. Like a nightmare they melted
away. The sun splashed back into Oliver's face and he
stumbled to his feet.

'Come quick! It's Fagin!' he called, but his voice was
trapped in his terrified throat. 'Come quick! Help!' he
shouted. And then, doubting the proof of his own eyes,
he leapt through the window and stared about him at an
empty garden.

They searched every bush and tree for Fagin or the

man with the crumpled face and the vivid red scar, but found no trace.

'I didn't dream it, truly!' cried Oliver. 'I'm not lying!'

'I believe you,' Rose Maylie assured him, but there was nothing to be done. The strange encounter so unnerved the boy, however, that Rose was determined at once to embark for London, to search out Mr Brownlow.

As the horse-cab pulled up outside the house in Pentonville, Oliver was dizzy with excitement. But all the windows were shuttered, and no one came to the door. He tried to squint between the blinds – at least to glimpse the beautiful portrait once more. But inside, everything was bare and empty and only shadows remained. Mr Brownlow and Mrs Bedwin had moved away.

'Do not abandon hope just yet,' Rose comforted Oliver. 'We shall put up at a hotel until we learn news of them. If they are still in the country, we shall find them, Oliver. My word on it.'

CHAPTER 12

in which Nancy is true to her word

'How are you feeling, Bill?' asked Nancy tenderly. It was the first time Sikes had woken for days. He had caught a cold and sunk into weeks of feverish illness. He was thin and pale. 'Weak as water, blast your eyes,' he croaked. 'Help me up off this bed. Get me a drink.'

After all her nights of watching and nursing Bill, Nancy was barely any stronger herself. 'There's nothing in the house. I went to Fagin for money, but 'til today, he's been out of town. "On business," the Artful Dodger says.'

'Well, get over there now and tell him I need ten pound. What's he think he's doing, going off and leaving me at death's door? He owes me. He'd be nothin' without me . . . Well? What you waiting for? The back of my hand?'

'Bill, be nice . . . ' implored Nancy. 'Haven't I looked after you all this while?'

'Oh and see if you can't find out what the old villain's been up to! "Business," my eye!' he spat.

At Fagin's kitchen, Nancy teased and cajoled, shouted and pleaded until Fagin advanced Bill five gold pounds.

She sat before the fire then, and seemed to doze – even when the man Monks arrived, and the other boys were turned out of the room. 'You've got news,' said Monks. 'News of Oliver?' He broke off, jerking his head in Nancy's direction.

'Who's that?'

'Don't mind her. Nancy's sound enough,' said Fagin. 'But we can discuss business up in my study if you prefer, my dear.'

The two climbed to a filthy box room on the floor above, and sat, heads close, swapping secrets. 'They've come to London, you say?' said Monks.

'That's right, my dear. Staying at the Feathers Hotel.'

'So you can snatch the boy back? You've done it before, devil roast him.'

'All in good time, my dear.' Fagin's voice dripped like oil. 'You should be thinking of that *proof* you spoke of. Where does the boy stand without *proof* of his identity? I've told you everything he said to me about his workhouse days, about the Beadle who took charge of him. Shouldn't you have words with this Beadle, Bumble, to lay hands on those . . . trinkets you spoke of? If they still exist. Trust me, your little brother will keep 'til you come again.'

Their footsteps on the stairs seemed to have roused Nancy from her doze, for they found her half way out of

her chair, pulling on her bonnet. She said goodnight to Fagin, wasting no more than a sideways glance on Monks. 'I must get back to Bill, or he'll give me what for,' she said. In the firelight, her eyes seemed unnaturally bright.

Bill Sikes noticed it too. 'You got the fever now?' he said, as she moved restlessly around the room preparing supper. 'You're no good to me sick, you know?'

Nancy gave a sharp, high laugh. 'Fever? Not me. Eat, Bill. I bought food. And gin. You should eat, now you're on the mend.'

He did eat, too, and greedily guzzled down the gin she poured. Suddenly he sat down on the bed, too sleepy even to curse, and slumped sideways on to the pillow. Instantly Nancy was in her coat and bonnet and running down the stairs.

Along the busy streets she ran, darting in front of horse-cabs and scattering knots of pedestrians who gaped after her. There was so little time! Soon the sleeping-draught she had put in Bill's gin would wear off. She had to run all the way, and even then she did not reach the Feathers Hotel until after nine.

'I must see Miss Rose Maylie!' she told the hall porter.

'She won't see your kind,' said the porter, looking Nancy up and down.

'I should think not!' the maids agreed. 'She's a *respectable* lady.'

'Don't matter what you think of me,' gasped Nancy. 'Tell her I'm here, and that a life depends on it!'

Grudgingly, sneeringly, they delivered the message, certain that Miss Maylie would send the scruffy girl away. But Rose Maylie had far more charity than they had. Even knowing nothing of Nancy, she offered at once to help her if she was able and got out her purse to do so.

'It's not money I'm after,' said Nancy. 'I've got news 'bout Oliver.'

'You know Oliver?' exclaimed Miss Maylie dropping her purse.

'I'm Nancy. I'm the one what snatched him from the old gentleman in Pentonville.'

If Rose was shocked, she hid it well. 'You had better sit down.'

'Do you know a man called Monks? No? Well, he knows you. And he knows young Oliver 'n' all! Just tonight I heard he was Oliver's brother!'

Nancy recounted everything she had overheard as she crouched, eavesdropping, on the stairs of Fagin's kitchen. She told how the man called Monks seemed to want Oliver ruined – not murdered, no, but gaoled or sunk deep in a life of crime – how Fagin might have managed it, too, but for the bungled robbery. 'My life's a wash-out and there's no saving me,' Nancy said at last, smearing the rouge[11] on her cheeks with the back of her hand as she wiped away her tears. 'But if Oliver's got a chance – some prospects in life – I won't stand by and see him robbed. And you must keep him safe, ma'am. Don't let Fagin get his claws into him again. I'll try to find out more, but I'm dead already, if my sweetheart sniffs out what I done.'

Rose Maylie assured Nancy that she would be perfectly safe. Why, once the gang was in prison, Nancy could make a fresh start, away from her sordid life, her

---

[11] Red face powder for colouring the cheeks.

evil cronies . . .

'No!' said Nancy. 'I won't desert my Bi- . . . my sweetheart. He may not be much, but he's all a girl like me gets given. No. I won't turn him in – nor testify against Fagin, which would be the same thing. I only come here tonight for Oliver's sake. If Monks gets hold of this "proof", whatever it is, I'll let you know. How? Somehow. Tell you what: a week today I'll walk on London Bridge between eleven and midnight. You may come and find me there . . . though God help me if my Bill ever gets wind of it . . . '

The visit left Rose Maylie shaken. She was heartily glad when news came to the hotel next morning: Mr Brownlow had been found! His new address had been tracked down. Now, at least, she would have an ally against London's shadowy, violent underworld.

The cab stopped outside a house in the Strand, and Rose Maylie went inside alone. The maid showed her to a parlour where two elderly gentlemen rose to greet her, polite but unsure why a beautiful young stranger should call on them unannounced. At the mention of Oliver's name, Mr Brownlow sat down and stood up again, and his friend Mr Grimwig swore he would eat his head if the boy was not bad through and through.

Briefly Rose told her story and, while she did so, saw Mr Brownlow glance time and time again at a portrait on the wall.

'I will, of course, do everything I can to help you, dear lady,' he said, when the story was ended, 'but first may I write to Oliver, perhaps, and send him my warmest regards?'

'Why not give them in person?' said Rose. 'Oliver is waiting downstairs.'

At that Mr Brownlow leapt from his chair and fairly bounded down the stairs – *'Mrs Bedwin! Great news! Come quickly!'* – and out of the house. Wrenching open the cab door, he clambered inside. Meanwhile, in the upstairs parlour, Mr Grimwig tipped his chair on to one leg and spun round in it three times before jumping up and planting a kiss on Miss Maylie's forehead, which was an *outrageous* thing to do.

CHAPTER 13

in which Monks lays hands on something not belonging to him

Mr Bumble began to think he had made a big mistake. Where was his tricorn hat now, or his staff-of-office? A parish beadle cuts a fine figure, with hat and cane, but a Master of the Workhouse? In his new line of work Mr Bumble was no longer so dignified, so imposing, so awe-inspiring. 'I sold myself for thirty teaspoons,' he thought. 'I did!'

And as for marriage . . . 'Are you sitting there still?' demanded Mrs Corney (now 'Mrs Bumble', of course.)

Mr Bumble decided to assert himself. 'I am *thinking*,' he said pompously.

'With half a brain? Nonsense. Stir yourself, you idle lummock. Get out of here and stop making the place untidy.'

Yes, romance had cooled considerably since that raw winter night when he had proposed to the workhouse Matron.

'I shall move when I'm good and ready,' said Bumble. 'A man is master in his own house, I hope!'

At that, Mrs Bumble burst into tears of rage.

Mr Bumble, determined to stand firm, said, 'Cry all you wish, madam! My soul is waterproof!'

Unfortunately, Mrs Bumble, far from showing wifely obedience, began slapping his head, punching his ears and pulling his hair. Mr Bumble was obliged to run. Along every passageway, he had to suffer the grins and jibes of the paupers, and their laughter behind his back. Mr Bumble was hen-pecked, and for such a man there is no remedy in the world . . . except the pub.

He did not drink alone, however. A man sat down opposite him – a young man but with an oddly colourless, twisted face and glaring eyes. 'Bumble the Beadle?' he asked.

'I was, sir, I was, until lately. Now I'm Warden of the Workhouse and, to my misfortune, Mrs Bumble is the Matron.'

'In that case, you both remember a boy called Oliver Twist.'

Once the boy's name was mentioned, Bumble would gladly have talked at length about the sinful, the vicious, the incomparably wicked Oliver Twist. But Monks was interested only in one day of Oliver's history – the day of his birth. 'Who was the midwife? Is she still living? Where can I find her?'

'Old Sally died last year,' Bumble told him.

'Aha! Then I am safe!'

'Yes, my own good lady was with her when she died . . . ' A memory glimmered in Bumble's head. Monks saw it there, in Bumble's eyes, and knew that old Sally had not gone silent to her grave. Scribbling an address on a piece of paper, he thrust it at Bumble. 'Come at midnight to this address. Bring your wife. I'll make it worth your while.'

There was thunder rolling around the sky by midnight, and rain, torrential rain. The piece of paper grew sodden in Mr Bumble's hand, and the ink letters bled. He and his bride gaped up at the dingy riverside building doubtfully. Their dislike of one another was momentarily forgotten in their curiosity and greed.

'You hold your tongue now,' snapped Mrs Bumble. 'Leave all the talking to me.'

Monks was greatly changed by the weather. Every flicker of lightning brought sweat rolling down his ashen face and he chewed on his twisted lip. While the thunder rolled, he could neither hear nor speak for sheer terror. By the light of a single lantern, the three sat around a small table, their heads almost touching. 'Well? Say what you know,' demanded Monks.

'First say what you are paying,' said Mrs Bumble uncowed even by Monks.

'Twenty pounds – if your information is worth having.'

'Make it twenty-five and you may judge for yourself.'

Coins clinked on to the table, their shine dulled in the gloom. Then Mrs Bumble recounted the night when old Sally had died, in the selfsame bed as Oliver's mother, weighed down by the guilt of a twelve-year-old crime.

As she spoke, the storm broke directly over the house. Monks became wildly agitated. *'Do you have it now? Did you take it from her? Did you bring it here?'* He was almost choking on his own fear.

The workhouse Matron drew out a parcel no bigger than a pocket watch and laid it on the table. Monks fell on it with both hands and with a cry of 'I have it!' clutched to him the only proof in the world of Oliver's identity.

CHAPTER 14

in which Nancy keeps her promise

The following week, crouched on the stairs outside Fagin's 'study', Nancy heard the triumph in Monks' voice. He had returned from his trip into the country, and she could tell at once that he had come back with the 'proof' he so craved and feared.

It was Sunday. Now, if she could just get away before midnight, she could keep her rendezvous with Rose Maylie on London Bridge. Nancy had no sleeping draught to put in Bill's drinks tonight, but perhaps she could simply slip out unnoticed.

After Monks had gone, Sikes and Fagin settled to an evening talking business. (At least Sikes settled to cursing and drinking, while the older man soothed and smoothed him like a crow preening a crocodile.) They paid no attention to Nancy.

Quietly she got up and put on her bonnet and shawl. Softly she crossed to the door and turned the handle.

'Where you going?' snarled Sikes.

'Just out for a walk, Bill. I need some air.'

'Stick yer head out the window, then,' said Bill.

Nancy, her nerves at breaking point, paced the room

wildly, first asking, then begging Bill to let her go. But the more eager she grew, the angrier and more obstinate Bill became. Finally, grabbing her by both arms, he forced her, sobbing and struggling, into a chair and pinned her there by brute force.

'I tell you, it's the fever,' he said to Fagin.

'Very likely, my dear,' said Fagin.

'Women! They take a thing into their heads and there's no telling them.'

'Just as you say, I'm sure,' said Fagin sweetly.

But unlike Sikes, who was aswill with gin, Fagin still had his wits about him. Long after Nancy had settled to silently weeping, Fagin still watched her with gimlet eyes, puzzling over her odd behaviour.

Next day, in his cellar-kitchen, Fagin gave the Artful Dodger his instructions. 'I want you to watch Nancy for me, Dodger, you hear? If she goes out alone, follow her. I believe she may have found herself a new sweetheart, and Bill wouldn't like that. Not one bit. You know how I hates disloyalty among our little band: so keep an eye, my dear. Keep an eye.'

The following Sunday, Nancy had no difficulty in getting away. Bill was out robbing a house and would not be back 'til morning. She hurried across London to where the oily blackness of the River Thames twisted and surged beneath a dreary span of lamp-lit stone.

Chill and dispirited after two hours of waiting, Rose Maylie and Mr Brownlow were about to go home. Twice they had come, and twice Nancy had not. Perhaps the girl had never intended to meet them. Perhaps she had only said it so as to be left in peace.

Then, as midnight struck, a hurrying figure came into view.

'So. The two of you have found each other, have you?' said Nancy, eyeing Mr Brownlow. She was plainly terrified. 'Pure dread come over me on my way here. I smelled blood and I saw a coffin passing when there was no coffin there . . . Still, it must be done.'

Like a traveller laying down a heavy pack, Nancy laid the news of Monks' return before them, his talk of proof, his triumphant delight in the packet he had bought from Bumble and the Matron.

'Describe this man Monks to me,' said Brownlow.

She did: his age, his twisted face, eyes so deep-set as to make his face like a skull.

'And on his neck . . . ' Brownlow prompted her.

'Yes! A vivid red mark! You know him, then! You do!'

Brownlow was cautious. 'There must be many such men in the world. I cannot be sure.'

'You poor girl!' said Rose, touching Nancy's hand. 'Won't you come home with us? Even now it is not too late to break free of these dreadful associates of yours.

I can see you are not like them – not truly wicked. Come away with us, now. There are places where you could be safe – where you could begin again!'

'No! Don't ask it! It may be wrong, but I'll never leave the man I love. He'll be the death of me, but I'll love him 'til the day I die. Save Oliver. Give him a chance in life! Find Monks if you can and take that proof off him. But as for me . . . I'll never give up on my Bill!' And she was gone, stumbling away, weeping.

Little did she know that, hidden in the well of the bridge steps, the Artful Dodger stood listening and had heard every word.

CHAPTER 15

in which Bill commits his greatest crime

Like wasps emerging from a nest, the words came slowly and haltingly out of the Artful Dodger's mouth and hovered in the air – terrible, fearful words that could never be unsaid. There were no jolly quips now, no comical poses. While Fagin held Sikes tight by the wrists, the Artful Dodger recounted his night's work.

Sikes howled like a soul in torment and wrenched free of Fagin. *'Let me go, curse you!'* He rushed wildly up the stairs, but the door was locked. *'Let me out!'*

'Bill! Bill! Just a word! A single word.' Toiling up the stairs, the thief master laid his hand on the lock. 'You won't be too ... violent, will you, Bill? Eh? Not too violent for our own personal safety, I mean.' They exchanged glances, and their eyes were both redder than hot coals, burning with the same vengeful hatred.

Fagin had let Sikes know of Nancy's treachery and the minutes of Nancy's life were surely ticking to a close.

There was blood on his clothes and blood on his hands. There were pictures etched on his brain, and words ringing in his ears like a church knell.

' . . . It's not too late, Bill! I never narked on you. I never would! Let's go away, Bill – out of this country – begin again and live better lives! The lady said to me, "It's not too late." It's never too late with God, if you're truly sorry!'

Well, he had made her truly sorry. Yeah, Nancy the traitor was truly sorry now. Leastways she would be if she weren't . . .

Every face he passed seemed to turn and peer at him; every pair of eyes seemed to be her eyes. The dawn came up blood red, red like her blood. *Clip-clip-clip* went the claws of his wretched dog, padding along behind. *Swish-swish* went the ghostly skirts of his ghostly sweetheart, following, all the time following . . .

Bill Sikes headed out of London. He walked and he walked, without knowing where he was going. Soon the body would be discovered – Nancy's body – and every policeman and Bow Street runner[12] would be searching for him. He had been rash. He ought to have hidden the body – got rid of it in the river or some place. But those eyes – those eyes had driven him out on to the streets, and those words clanging in his ears, *'I love you, Bill! No, Bill! Let me live! I love you!'*

A salesman in an inn was selling patent soap, *'Gets out every kind of stain, speck, spot or spatter! Wine stains, fruit stains, beer stains, paint stains, pitch stains, blood stains*

---

[12] A London policeman.

... Here's a stain on this gentleman's hat – blood by the looks of it – a butcher are you, sir? – But with this soap I can . . . '

Bill snatched the hat with a curse, and fled the inn.

Outside stood the morning mail coach. The driver was saying, 'I heard tell there was a murder in the City – a woman. Bad do . . . a man with a dog. They're looking for a man with a dog.'

Away plunged Sikes into the woods, away from the sound of that word 'murder' and all those eyes . . . That noise again! That swish of skirts, that woman's soft tread! It must be the dog stirring up the dry leaves. Wretched animal! Everyone knew Sikes by that animal. That dog would be the death of him.

'Come here, you brute!' called Sikes. He wrapped a heavy stone in a handkerchief: he would tie it round the dog's neck and drown the creature in that pond. 'Come here, I said!' The loyal dog wagged its tail and trotted closer – but squirmed away as Bill made a grab for it, and ran off into the wood. Sikes threw a stone after it. 'Keep away from me, you hear?'

By midday, the newspapers had news of the murder. Some said the murderer had fled abroad.

'Suppose I go back to London?' thought Sikes. 'That's the last place they'll think to look for me. I'll hole up on Jacob Island. Must find that brat Oliver and cut his throat, for old time's sake. After a week or two, Fagin can

help me get to France.' And he retraced his steps with
nothing for company now but the *swish-swish* of those
ghostly skirts and in every knothole of every tree those
eyes, glaring and accusing.

Skulking along at a distance, bound by a leash of
loyalty, the house-breaker's dog kept pace with him, but
out of sight – at a safe distance – unseen. Sikes had
shown it nothing but cruelty, but had beaten into it the
habit of perfect, dogged devotion.

Jacob Island was a filthy muddy backwater of the Thames at Rotherhithe – a ditch full at high tide and, at low tide, a foul-smelling sewer. Its warehouses stood abandoned, roofless, and lived in only by rats. Broken-down houses teetered out over the water, rotting galleries, boarded up windows. Society's most hopeless and helpless holed up here and hauled up the muddy water to drink. It was the last bolt-hole of every beggar and thief.

Naturally, it was to this joy-forsaken wilderness that Bill Sikes took himself.

Meanwhile, Fagin's kitchen of thieves shifted ground. The appalling murder, the secrets spilled by Nancy made it necessary for the wipe-swipers[13] to scatter.

'Keep out of sight, my dears,' said Fagin, panic-stricken by the sudden rash of policemen combing the London streets. 'Find some safe crib out of sight of the Law. After, when the heat is off, we shall find one another again, never fear!' And some of Fagin's boys also made tracks for Jacob Island.

It was on his way to the island that the Artful Dodger took it into his head to pick one last pocket before going to ground. A promising target tottered into view, and the Artful Dodger had no trouble rifling his pockets. The shame was that he gained only a cheap snuff box by it. The greater shame was that a policeman tugged his

---

[13] Someone who steals handkerchiefs; a pick pocket.

collar, and the Artful Dodger was well and truly nabbed. Of all the thoughts that pass through a boy's head at such a time, the one that troubled Dodger most was to be arrested for the sake of a tuppeny-ha'penny snuff box rather than a gold watch.

Quicker than even the Artful Dodger could credit, his trial was fixed. The great, the renowned, the flash master of petty theft was all but on his way to the convict colonies of Australia.

Toby Crackitt and Kags both headed for Jacob Island, too – for the topmost gallery of the tallest house. Its downstairs front windows and door were lined with iron sheets to keep out unwelcome visitors, but they climbed in by a back window. This was a favourite crib of Fagin's boys in times of trouble.

Halfway through the afternoon there was a scrabbling and a thump and in at the window jumped a dog – Sikes' dog – filthy and exhausted, its paws red raw from walking.

Three hours later, there was a hammering at the door. Thinking it was Charlie Bates or the Artful Dodger, Kags opened the door. Then that fiend was in among them – Bill Sikes – and they were too terrified to say a word.

'Newspapers say Fagin's took!' said Sikes. 'Is it true?'

'It is,' said Toby. 'He went back to the kitchen to fetch his treasures. But the Law was keeping watch and they followed him in. He tried to hide up the chimney, but his legs were too long and he got took.'

Just then, the dog crawled forward to lick his master's hand.

'What's that brute doing here?' Sikes was aghast at the sight of the dog.

The boys could only shrug. 'Must've guessed where you'd come,' mumbled Kags.

Then Charlie Bates arrived.

He saw his mates curled up against the wall, meekly answering Sikes' questions. He could see they were in fear of their lives. But Charlie, his heart still full of grief for the dead Nancy, lost all self-control. He hurled himself at Sikes and began pummelling at him, biting and kicking, and calling for the others to help him. 'You know what he did! He killed her! I'll give him up to the Law even if they boil him in oil for it!'

Too terrified to help, Kags and Toby would have watched Charlie killed in front of their very eyes but for a great surging noise in the streets below. It signalled the arrival of a thousand people. The murderer's dog had been seen. The neighbourhood was in full cry!

'Get me a rope!' said Sikes. 'The tide's in. I'll let myself down into the water at the back of the house and swim out. They won't take me! Not before I've slit the throat of that Oliver Twist, rot him! Get me a rope, blast your eyes, or I'll do three more murders here and now!'

Thrown into an alcove like an old sack, Charlie Bates prised open the window and, insanely brave in his

hatred, shouted down to the crowd below, *'He's up here! Come and take him! The murderer's here!'*

The rope was knotted round the chimney pot. It dangled down into the foetid ditch. All the while Sikes was climbing onto the roof, Charlie Bates was shrieking, *'He's getting away! The back of the house! Go round to the back!'*

Every muddy alleyway, every filthy lane was packed with people baying for Sikes' blood. Theft was one thing. Murder was different. Sikes had murdered one of their own kind: a poor girl, a common girl, a harmless, kind-hearted, popular, powerless girl, and they hated him for it.

Besides, an elderly gentleman, newly arriving by hackney cab, was offering a reward of fifty pounds for the murderer's capture. Mr Brownlow had come to see Nancy avenged, and his offer roused the crowd to even greater excitement.

Still the man on the roof might escape. Knotting the rope into a noose, Bill prepared to loop it round his body, to make the climb down into the swilling water. His dog scrambled after him onto the tiles, whimpering, ignored.

Where did Sikes look in that last fateful moment? Was it at the clouds or down into the street, into the river or at the teetering slums opposite? Wherever it was, he saw there the same eyes that had haunted him through suburbs, countryside and town, the eyes that would carry him all the way down to Hell.

'The eyes again!' he shrieked, and missing his footing, fell from the roof. The rope went taut. The knot ran up tight – not round his body, for he had not the time to loop it under his arms – but round his throat. Bill Sikes hanged, as surely as if justice had taken its right and natural toll.

CHAPTER 16

Trials and errors

When Mr Brownlow and Rose Maylie found out that one of Fagin's boys was on trial, they hurried down to the courthouse. The boy might just know where Monks was to be found. Oliver begged to go, too, saying that Jack Dawkins had been a friend to him and probably needed someone close by to comfort him.

In fact the Artful Dodger was in fine fettle. Before the sun sank for ever on his magnificent career, he was determined to put on a show that befitted the renowned Artful Dodger. The court was crowded – so crowded that Brownlow could get nowhere near the dock. The Artful Dodger appeared, dressed as usual in his oversized coat and jaunty top hat, blustering and filibustering like a bantam cock.

'I demand to know why I am placed in this disgraceful situation! I am an Englishman! I have rights!'

'Silence there!' cried the gaoler.

'What is this case?' asked the magistrate.

'Pick-pocketing, your worship.'

'Where are the witnesses?'

'You might well ask! That's what I'd like to know!'

brayed the Artful Dodger. 'Where are they indeed, and how dare they defame a man of my character?'

The crowd gave a whoop of delight. Here was a prisoner with style!

'What have you to say in your defence?' asked the magistrate lamely.

'Are you addressing me, squire?'

'Have you anything to say against your accusers?'

'Nope! I wouldn't stoop to holding a conversation with the villains.'

'So you mean to say nothing in your defence?'

'What, here? Never! Not in front of this low class of justice!' The crowd gave a cheer. 'Now when I next take breakfast with my friend the Prime Minister . . . '

'Send him down!' ordered the magistrate.

'What, the Prime Minister?' gasped the Artful Dodger in shocked tones.

The crowd in court gave a shriek of laughter.

'Come along with me!' said the gaoler.

'Oh I will, I will, and its no good you begging me to stay! I'm ashamed to be mixing with the hoi polloi[14] on this bench. No! No good begging my forgiveness! I wouldn't go free now, not if you begged me. Here! Carry me off to prison, gaoler! Take me away!'

The court by this time was in uproar – people cheering, people hooting, ladies blowing kisses to the young boy. The going down of the Artful Dodger was as glorious as any sinking sun.

Oliver tugged on Mr Brownlow's coat. 'What will become of him?'

'He will be put on a ship to Australia, child, along with other thieves like him.'

Oliver bit his lip. 'I hope he likes Australia,' he said, then turned to Rose. 'Perhaps he will grow sheep and get very rich and be a swell in Australia.'

'I would not be at all surprised,' said Rose comfortingly.

---

[14] The ordinary people.

The mood of the court had changed now, for Fagin was being brought in. It took an army of policemen to protect him from the anger of the crowd; somehow they had found out that Fagin was a party to Nancy's death, and would have torn him limb from limb if they could have laid hands on him. This time is was the judge's turn to be cheered, as he condemned Fagin to hang.

As Fagin was dragged away to the condemned cell, a young man with a twisted white face and a vivid red scar on his neck pushed his way towards the door. Monks was feeling relieved. At least Fagin had not had time to name his acquaintances. As Monks barged his way through the crush he collided with Oliver. At the sight of the boy he stared, mad-eyed, and foam burst from between his lips. *'Rot your bones! I should have had the courage to kill you! I should! I will! Black death upon your heart, you –* ' He raised a fist as if to hit Oliver . . . but fell to the ground, writhing and groaning in a fit.

Oliver gazed down at him. 'It is the man at the window!'

'Oh yes,' said Mr Brownlow. 'I know this particular young man all too well.'

Orders were given for Monks to be put in a hackney cab and carried to Mr Brownlow's house. There, with the door locked on the outside, an interview took place that changed several lives.

At first, Monks was silent and surly. 'I cannot imagine what business you think you have with me, but I am certain I have none with you.'

'If you will not talk, then I shall have to tell your story for you,' said Mr Brownlow. 'There was once a man whose family persuaded him to marry young: not for love, but for money. Love? There was never any love in that marriage. Before long there was nothing but bitterest hatred. A son was born, but soon afterwards, the wife deserted her husband and went abroad in search of a sweeter life. Years passed. Believing that his wife was dead and thinking himself free, he dared to hope for some happiness. He dared to fall in love and marry again. Let us call his sweetheart . . . Agnes.

Imagine his grief and horror, then, when he found that his wife – his first wife, I mean – was not dead at all! At once he left for Europe to find her and to beg for a divorce. While he was in Rome, he caught a fever – a fever he knew would be the death of him.'

'Your story is long and tedious,' said Monks. 'Why are you telling me all this. Unlock the door and let me go.'

'Oh, would you rather I called a policeman and told it to him? The choice is yours.'

At that, Monks slumped back in his chair scowling horribly. 'As I was saying . . . ' continued Mr Brownlow. 'The man died of a fever in Rome . . . but not before he could make a will. He shared his property equally between his two children – the son living with his first wife, and the unborn child of his beloved Agnes. Shall I tell you how I know? *Because he posted it to me!* Agnes, you see, was my niece!'

Rose Maylie fell back with a start. 'These people are known to you, Mr Brownlow?'

'Known to me. Loved by me. But of course the letter came too late to help poor dear Agnes. Through no fault of hers, she found herself expecting a child and not truly married. So she ran away, to save her family from the scandal. She got only as far as W —— N before her baby arrived. That baby, sir was your brother, Oliver! Call yourself by whatever false name you choose, you are Edward Leeson, the firstborn of those sons, and Oliver is the secondborn. He is entitled to half of everything your father left, but you – *you, sir* – wanted it all, didn't you?'

In the corner of the room, Oliver sat very still, white-faced, spellbound by a life story about people he had never met or heard of before. What was his name doing in such a story?

'You knew that if Oliver was in prison or sunk in a life of crime, he could not inherit. How happy you must have been, on your return to England, to discover that Oliver was already in the grips of your friend Fagin! You urged Fagin to turn the boy into a criminal. But his nature was too honest, was it not? Too good and too honest!'

'*I have no brother! You have no proof!*' protested Monks, wiping the sweat from his red throat.

'You may think so, sir. You went to great pains to buy back what proof there was, from the Matron of the Workhouse where Oliver was born. A locket and a wedding ring, was it not? You bought them for just twenty-five pounds, didn't you? This much I learned on a visit to the treacherous Mr and Mrs Bumble! And you entrusted the parcel to Fagin, to keep among his ill-gotten 'treasures'. This much I learned from poor dead Nancy!'

Now, for the first time, Monks looked at Oliver – not as a brother might look, but as if he were some dog that had tracked him over a thousand miles and could not be shaken off. 'I could have killed you, but I feared your ghost would haunt me! *I should have killed you when I had the chance!*'

CHAPTER 17

in which our characters make their farewells

It was very dark. Fagin screamed for a light. He cursed and raved. He howled, and tore his hair. 'Light! More light!' The clocks struck. The days seemed to pass in minutes. The nights dragged by without sleep.

On the last day, several boys came to the prison gate and asked if a reprieve had come for the prisoner, but none had and the boys went away. At dawn on Monday Oliver and Mr Brownlow knocked at the prison gate and were let in.

'This is no place for a child,' said the warder.

'I know,' said Mr Brownlow, 'but our business concerns this boy's future life: he has to be here.'

In his prison cell, Fagin sat rocking to and fro, muttering to himself.

'Fagin?' said the guard.

'That's me!' cried Fagin. 'A very old, old man!'

'Here's someone wants to ask you some questions.'

At the sight of Oliver, Fagin shrank back into the corner. 'Put that child to bed, Dodger, do!'

Mr Brownlow asked him about the locket and ring, but the old thief-master only answered, 'It's a lie! It's all a lie! Come here, Oliver and let me whisper to you!'

Unafraid, Oliver let go of Mr Brownlow's hand and went forward. 'Shall I say a prayer with you, Mr Fagin?' he asked.

'My treasures, Oliver,' he whispered, his red beard scratchy against Oliver's ear. 'All those treasures I saved up for my old age? They are up in the chimney. We must go and get them, you and I. You hold my hand and we'll walk out of here. Steady now. They'll let us pass when they see you. Everybody trusts you, Oliver. You have an honest face.' He pushed Oliver towards the door.

He was quite mad of course. The guards grabbed him, and Mr Brownlow hurried Oliver away.

They went at once to Fagin's kitchen and there,

among the baubles and knickknacks, the snuffboxes and seven gold watches, the tie pins and tiaras and rings, they found a locket and a wedding ring. Inside the ring was engraved the name 'Agnes'. Inside the locket were a lock of hair and the picture of a young woman with yellow hair.

'It is the pretty lady in the portrait!' cried Oliver. 'But how?'

'Agnes was my niece, child,' said Mr Brownlow. 'When I first saw your face, all those unhappy memories came flooding back – young Leeson dead in Rome, poor Agnes shamed and lost through no fault of her own . . . I did not realize it at the time, but it was your likeness to your dear, sweet mother that spoke to me that first day, when they tried you as a thief.'

Oliver's hand closed around the locket. Perhaps that was why the picture had struck such a chord in his heart. 'Agnes,' he whispered. 'Mother.'

For the first time in his life, Oliver held something that had belonged to his mother, something his mother had meant him to have. It made him want to cry.

'Your half brother – the man you call Monks – how should we deal with him do you think? He tried to ruin your life. He caused you to be shot.'

Oliver considered the matter earnestly. 'We should do as my father wished.'

Oliver's forgiving words delighted Mr Brownlow. 'Then so we shall! Your father's inheritance shall be split between you. Six for Edward and six for Oliver.'

'*Six pounds?*' gasped Oliver, staggered at the thought of such riches.

In his entire life he had only owned one penny.

'Six *thousand* pounds,' laughed Brownlow. 'Not a great sum, but since I mean to adopt you as my own son, you will not need so very much.'

Taking his six thousand pounds, Edward Leeson went abroad, lost all his money gambling, and ended life in prison.

Mr and Mrs Bumble, exposed as dishonest and untrustworthy, lost their posts as Master and Matron of the Workhouse. In fact they ended their days in the workhouse, and so came to experience the same joy and tenderness those in their charge had always felt. Mr Bumble's only comfort was that, once inside the workhouse, man and wife cannot live together and must say goodbye forever.

Rose Maylie married a clergyman and moved (with her aunt) to a pretty rectory deep in the countryside. Mr Brownlow and Oliver moved to a little cottage nearby, and Mr Grimwig came too, saying he would eat his head if he was going to let Brownlow have all the fun.

In the church alongside the rectory, a monument was

built in pure white marble, by order of Mr Oliver Twist
Leeson Brownlow. On it was a brass plate with just one
word: AGNES.

As for the rest of Fagin's boys, they slipped away into
the dirty dark of London's vastness, to sink or swim as
best they could, having nowhere else to go and no one
to fend for them, no one to care if they lived or died.